ZACHARY STEPHEN

Meditative Movement

How to unlock your inner self through mindful movement

Contents

1

Introduction

Welcome to Meditative Movement! I'm so excited to share this journey with you and help you discover why it is you purchased this book in the first place. What is it that spoke to you? Why are you here? Do you feel stagnant in your goals and every day life? Are you wanting to dive deeper into your personal journey? Do you wish you had more time to focus on yourself, could improve your health both inner and outer, or gain more confidence in your own personal strengths? These are things I think about all the time. In today's world, it's extremely challenging to even want to dive deeper into self improvement let alone take the action necessary to get there. Life is full of such a wide variety of stresses, distractions, and general anxiety that a lot of us neglect some simple things that can make it all a bit more manageable. That's why I've decided to write this book.

So, who am I? My name is Zachary Stephen and I've spent a large majority of my 38 years here on earth searching. Searching for what exactly? I guess just about anything and everything. From a very early age I was always a very interested and fascinated individual. I wanted to know about and question everything, from religion to sports, music to politics, travel, food, finance, history and the list goes on. As healthy as it might sound to explore curiosity, that constant searching gave me a lack of association and identity. I had no group and no belonging. When traumatic grief invaded my life at a very young age, it sent me into a sort of spiral. I gained weight, ignored my needs, got lazy and stagnant. I spent several years being a person that I didn't want to be until I fell back in love with the joy of movement. And not just movement but how that movement can unlock a calming peaceful meditative quality within. Through all of my experiences, it's the one thing that has kept me grounded and moving forward (pun intended) with a lightness and positive mentality helping me gain perspective on the challenges and stresses of daily life. In this book, I'd like to share with you some of those experiences and hopefully make you excited to start the journey of being your best self.

This is not a book for fitness gurus, advanced yogis, or future monks. This is a book for the everyday person that may be fearful of the word meditation or the commitment to an exercise routine. This is a book for people wanting to make lifestyle changes forever, not start the hottest fad diet or join a new gym. This is a book for people curious about unlocking a true love for connecting mind and body to be your best self for you and those you love. This is a book that will show you that meditation and movement don't have to be scary and are actually extremely accessible to all persons, body types, ages, and backgrounds. This is a book for you.

2

What is Meditation and Why Do We Need It?

So let's start with the most obvious question. What is Meditation? There's so much material out there on meditation. Books, YouTube, Religion, New Age Influencers; it seems like everywhere we turn these days people are pushing an idealized version of what meditation should be. Well I have a strong opinion about that. I'll say meditation is **Anything You Want It To Be**. "What? That's impossible. There's obviously specific types of meditation." Well of course there is but hear me out. Meditation is about a goal more that a specific practice. In my opinion, that goal is about working towards a clear mind and calming your spirit. Meditation should be about how you feel and what you're getting out of it. Do you feel rejuvenated? Do you feel relaxed? Do you feel like you've improved your equilibrium? If the answer is yes to those questions, then you can consider it meditation.

Meditation can be going for a walk or hike, cooking a recipe from scratch, taking on some sort of artistic endeavor. Anything that allows you to have a singular focus, free yourself of stress, and gives you a brief moment of detachment from daily pressures I would consider meditation. It doesn't have to be guided by someone more advanced than you or feel like work. Meditation should be about you and only you. A brief moment to do nothing but look within and check in with yourself. Check in with your mind. Check in with your body.

I've dabbled in all sorts of meditation, my first arguably being Christian prayer. Even though organized religion was ultimately not for me, prayer was one of the first times I was taught to exist within. In those moments of prayer, I was supposed to clear my mind and focus on my connection with God. I hold a lot of value in those early years of my life even if I still don't identify as a Christian. I do identify as spiritual, and prayer is a big part of that foundation. Since then I've taken years of martial arts, years of yoga, meditated in Buddhist Temples, ran thousands of miles, played drums for thousands of hours, lifted weights, followed specific exercise regiments, hiked multiple days at 14,000 ft to Machu Picchu, and tons of other things I consider meditative practice. In all of those moments, I spend the time focusing on the activity at hand and getting lost in it. Truly living in the moment and focusing on breath, I consider every one of these activities meditation and I feel better about myself every time I'm in these moments.

So, how does meditation improve your life? In the fast-paced and constantly evolving world we live in, finding moments of stillness and calm is an essential tool for personal growth and well being. One of the most potent tools in this quest is meditation. It can impact so many areas of your life from enhancing mental clarity to fostering emotional resilience and promoting physical health.

The practice of meditation provides a sanctuary for your mind among the chaos of daily life. It's a moment of solitude and pause in which you can disconnect from the external noise and realign with your inner self. Meditation is like a workout for your mind. Just like regular physical exercise expands the muscles in your body, consistent meditation expands your mental capacity. With Sustained attention to repetitive rhythmic breath, a mantra, or awareness of the sensations in your body, you train your mind to stay focused and present. This enhanced focus spills over into your everyday responsibilities, wants, and needs making you more productive and efficient.

Meditation will also have a positive impact on your emotional resilience. I mentioned grief being a big part of what started me on this journey. When I was 18 years old, my father was killed in a snow mobile accident, thrown off after hitting a tree and bleeding to death in my arms for about 2 hours. It was exactly as traumatic as it sounds and has defined every waking moment of my life since. With therapy and a lot of meditation I've been able to get to the point that I can see all the positive aspects that moment has had on me and the person I've become. Life's challenges can feel overwhelming and stress takes a full toll on our emotional well being. Meditation acts as a buffer against this stress. It encourages you to be more aware of your thoughts and emotions, helping you manage them in a healthier way. Feel your feelings, be open to them, and let them pass without controlling you. Meditation will equip you with a new set of tools to better face life's ups and downs with grace and resilience reminding you that you are strong and able to handle whatever comes your way.

The American Psychological Association (APA) published an article in 2019 stating, "Researchers reviewed more than 200 studies of mindfulness among healthy people and found mindfulness-based therapy was especially effective for reducing stress, anxiety and depression.(1)" By fostering mindfulness and self compassion, meditation helps you gain control over your emotional responses. It allows you to step back from negative thought patterns which in turn creates a more positive and balanced outlook on life. And even the simple fact that you just completed a self bettering activity can immediately make you feel a sense of pride and well being.

Extending beyond the mind, meditation can also be linked to improved physical health, such as lowered blood pressure, reduced inflammation, and enhanced immune function (2,3). Regular practice can contribute to a healthier heart and a stronger, more resilient body. Especially when mixed with the movement of your body, the health benefits start to become self evident. This is not about losing weight or getting ripped. This is about true long term functional health and giving yourself the best chance at aging with endurance, flexibility, strength, and peace of mind. Health has become such a hot topic in our culture that there is a lot of misinformation and get ripped (or get someone else rich) quick schemes. Health is not about a six pack or the perfect butt. Health is functional and long term and that's the goal we're seeking to achieve in this book.

Your personal growth through mediation can also have a positive impact on your relationships. By becoming more self aware and emotionally stable, you're better equipped to communicate and connect with the people you care about. Compassion and empathy often blossom from meditative practice, leading to deeper, more meaningful connections and relationships. If you've ever heard the saying, "you can't love someone else until you love yourself" then you understand the benefits here. Meditation will help you truly discover not only who you are but also gain perspective on why other people are who they are. By truly showing up and being there for ourselves we can then begin to give the same to those around us and dive deeper into those relationships.

Ultimately, meditation is a journey of self discovery. As you dive into your inner world, you will gain insight into your values, desires, and beliefs. This newfound self awareness can guide you in making more authentic life choices and pursuing a path that aligns with your true self.

One of the most important things to remind yourself on this journey is to maintain achievable goals. What does that mean? Well, that's for you to figure out. We're all coming from a different background of experience and physicality. What is right for your neighbor is likely not going to be right for you. Set achievable goals. If you've never run, don't tell yourself you're going to run a marathon, tell yourself you're going to run for 20 minutes 3 times a week. If you want to ingrain meditation and movement into your life, do it in a way that works for your body and your schedule. You shouldn't be too comfortable but you shouldn't be too uncomfortable either. Find that equilibrium of challenging yourself while keeping it attainable. You have your whole life for slow steady improvement. Remember, we're working on lifelong changes and to always be making progress. Progress on ourselves, our minds, our bodies, and our spirits. There is no end game, no finish line. True awareness is a constantly evolving actuality.

3

The Over Active Mind

Dealing with Distractions and Quieting the Inner Critic

Meditation is a powerful tool for cultivating inner peace and mental clarity, but for those of us with overactive minds, it can often feel like an uphill battle. The constant chatter in our head, that never ending random stream of thoughts, can make the idea of stillness seem impossible. However, it's essential to understand that meditation can be extremely beneficial for individuals with overactive minds and help calm the storm within. This chapter will explore some strategies for dealing with distractions and achieving a quieter mind during your meditation practice.

The first step and most important thing you can do to tame your overactive mind is acknowledge the incessant chatter. Trying to fight it can be a true exercise in futility. Instead of losing a battle trying to fight against it, simply recognize it as part of your mental process. Trying to suppress or eliminate theses thoughts can often backfire, making them more prominent and even louder than they started off. Our goal is to reshape our thinking and view these thoughts as clouds passing through the sky of your consciousness. Observe them, feel them for a brief moment, refrain judgment and let them slowly pass and dissipate into nothing. The more we let ourselves experience freely, the closer we get to getting rid of the noise all together. But try to snuff it out and you might be pouring water on a grease fire, instead just let them burn themselves out and you'll be making progress.

One approach for managing distractions is to practice focused meditation techniques. Concentration exercises, such as focused breath work can act as an anchor for your attention and reduce the chances of your mind wandering. When you start to notice distracting thoughts, gently guide your focus back to your anchor. The consistent redirecting of your attention can help you become less entangled in the chatter and foster a more tranquil state of mind. Something extremely simple that has always worked for me is box breath. Take a deep breath in for three counts, hold for three counts, breath out for three counts, hold for three counts, and repeat ad long as you can. It doesn't get more attainable than that. A simple box breath exercise is a great entry into meditative practice. It can be done on its own or in conjunction with a physical activity such as running, just swap breaths for steps.

Humans have been exploring different breathing techniques for centuries to achieve heightened or enlightened states of being. Feel free to explore what can work for you. There's more intense versions like Lion's breath or Wim Hof or relaxing focuses like mindful breathing that just hones in on the awareness of the natural rhythm of instinctual breath. It's always about finding what works for you and helps push you closer to your goals.

If all that sounds great and you still struggle to turn off the noise, guided meditation might be right for you. Guided meditations tend to be led by experienced practitioners or instructors who provide verbal cues, directives, and occasionally the right soundtrack to keep your mind on track. These sessions can provide structure and guidance, making it easier to navigate the labyrinth of thought. This journey doesn't have to be a completely solo endeavor. Guided meditation isn't for everyone but absolutely perfect for some. There are a lot of very good videos of all types on YouTube that can get you started. There's absolutely no requirement to spend money or join an in person group if that's not for you. Find what fits and lean into it.

One of the loudest distractions we hear is often our own inner critic. It is a relentless voice within us that drains and exacerbates our overactive minds. It's the part of us that self doubts, criticizes, and magnifies our flaws. Quieting the inner critic is a crucial aspect of meditation for those of us who struggle with an overly active mind. Meditation offers a unique opportunity to cultivate self compassion. As you sit in stillness, practice extending kindness and understanding to yourself. When your inner critic comes into the picture shouting at you with self judgment, acknowledge it and then gently shift your focus to compassion. Remind yourself that it's okay to have a wandering mind or to struggle with focus. Just as you'd be kind and patient with a friend, treat yourself with the same gentleness. Treating ourselves, with kindness, gentleness, and compassion will create a foundation that helps us extend those qualities to others and over time, quiet our own self critic.

During meditation, consider labeling your thoughts as the arise. When self critical or judgmental thoughts surface, label them as "judgment" or "self criticism." This simple act of labeling can create a separation between you and your thoughts. It allows you to observe these thoughts with less attachment and over time can diminish their power. The same can be said in the real world when you aren't practicing meditation. When you feel anger, pain, sadness, regret, disappointment; we can use this labeling technique to recognize them for what they are and remind ourselves not to be consumed by them. Feel it. Let it go.

Instead of leaning into the labels of judgment and self criticism, integrate positive affirmations into your practice. Repeating affirmation like "I am enough," "I am strong," "I am worthy of love," "I am worthy of compassion," "I accept myself as I am," can counteract the negative self talk perpetuated by your inner critic. Affirmations can gradually replace destructive thought patterns with healthier ones.

Meditation can also be a pathway to better sleep. Restless nights tend to result from racing thoughts and worries. Meditation can help you manage these internal and external interruptions and improve your sleep. Consider incorporating a brief evening meditation into your daily routine. This practice can help you unwind and quiet your mind before bed, making it easier to transition into restful sleep. Focus on breathing and releasing the day's stress and concerns. When you find yourself awake in the middle of the night, instead of turning on the TV or looking at your phone, go back to focusing on mindful breathing. Concentrate on your breath, inhale and exhale slowly and deeply. This wonderful and simple technique can bring you back to a state of relaxation making it easier to fall back asleep. Also try focusing on a true bedtime ritual. Create a calming routine that incorporates meditation and breath work. Over time, this consistency can signal to your body that it's time to wind down and help minimize interruptions in your sleep patterns.

The overactive mind is regularly accompanied by generalized worry and anxiety. Meditation is an important tool in addressing the issues and fostering a sense of tranquility. We've touched on mindfulness meditation, the act of focusing on and becoming aware of the natural rhythm and movement of the breath, and it's again relevant here. It inherently encourages being present in the moment, observing your thoughts and feelings, working towards non-judgment. Regular practice helps develop a more detached and non-reactive relationship with your thoughts.

Visualization techniques are another meditation method to help redirect your thoughts and manage anxiety and stress. Imagery meditations can transport you to a serene and calming place in your mind, providing an escape from intrusive thoughts. Focusing on honing your sends to create a more vivid and immersive experience. Put yourself in your ideal environment and really start to build a 3D 360 degree space of comfort and solitude. Maybe it's a real place from your past like your grandmother's kitchen. Notice the light, the sounds, the smells and engage your senses around you. Maybe it's a fantasy place that you can go to that is completely yours and yours alone. A cabin in an enchanted mountain forest with the perfect cracking fire and a light snow fall. Whatever your sanctuary is, build it meticulously and slowly. Adding more details every time you revisit until it truly becomes an accessible escape.

Grounding exercises like body scans or focusing on physical sensations, can help anchor you in the present moment and are one of my personal favorite ways to develop awareness. Directing your attention to the physical sensations of your body can shift your focus away from anxious thoughts and regain a sense of control. start from your toes and slowly work up your body checking in with every joint, muscle, appendage, and every other part of your body all the way up and out the top of your head. You can work your way back down or just continue to repeat the process. By drawing attention and focus to these micro areas, our bodies become more connected over time. You'll start to be aware of the very intricate highway system that makes up a complete you and unlock the joy of mind body connection.

This chapter could be the entire book in itself but these are just some of the ways regular meditation practice can transform your mindset first and physical self second. Worst case scenario, you're forcing yourself to just take a little solitude and reflect on all the things affecting you in the moment. Having an overactive mind is not a hindrance to meditation but rather an opportunity for growth and transformation. By acknowledging distractions, silencing your inner critic, managing sleep interruptions, and addressing worry and anxiety, you can begin to harness the power of meditation to find inner calm and peace; even in the midst of mental turbulence. The journey may be challenging but the rewards of a quieter, more tranquil mind, are well worth the effort.

4

Finding Balance

The Juggle of Life, Work, Kids, Relationships, Intimacy, Social Activity, You Time

Life can often feel like a delicate juggling act with numerous responsibilities and commitments vying for your attention. So many things are fighting for our attention every single day that sometimes we forget we have the power to choose where our attention goes and who or what we give it to. Far too often we neglect attention to ourselves first. Finding balance is essential to living a fulfilling and harmonious life.

Balancing work and person life is a perpetual challenge. To maintain equilibrium, it is ideal to set boundaries around your work hours. Create a dedicated workspace and separate work from home life. Prioritize your tasks and be assertive in communicating your needs with your colleagues. Regularly remind yourself that work is just one part of your life and it should not overshadow the rest. Of course these concepts are easier said than done. A lot of times we don't feel secure enough to set those boundaries or say no when it isn't in our best interest. Or we won't get the promotion we're hoping for if we don't put in extra hours and sacrifice our own personal lives. There's no magic solution but just that simple act of reminding yourself to hold space for life outside of work can help shed some of the stress. Jobs aren't forever, careers aren't forever, your relationship with yourself is the only thing that will be with you to the end. Be ambitious and work hard for what you want in life but don't let that ambition come at the sacrifice of your relationships, with others and yourself.

Parenting is a full-time job in itself and managing it alongside other commitments can be the most overwhelming thing imaginable. This is not a book on parenting as many with more knowledge than me have written countless words on the topic, but this is a reminder to schedule the part of you that is a parent just like you do the part that is a professional or spouse or friend. Organize a family schedule and involve your children in daily tasks and responsibilities where possible. Quality time with your kids is paramount and focus on meaningful interactions over quantity can really make the most out of the time that you spend together. Creating rituals out of all our habits and responsibilities creates a connection to the meaning behind them. Parenting is a ritual, maybe one of the oldest, and meditation can be a part of that ritual. Sitting down and working on calming breath work with children has shown to help deal with anxiety even in adolescence. It's never too early to share the joys and power of meditation with our kids!

Nurturing relationships of all types, whether with a partner, family, or friends, requires time and effort. Allocating time for regular check-ins, date nights or social gatherings can help maintain healthy connections. Open communication is key as it allows you to express your needs and listen to the needs of others. Sticking to schedules and creating boundaries helps compartmentalize all the things fighting for our attention. Organizing our responsibilities in little individual mental boxes creates an environment of direct connection with each activity and obligation. We owe it to ourselves to find a way to fulfill all our needs and live a complete life.

When bombarded with the pressure of careers and parenting we tend to put things like social activities, intimacy with our partners, and you time on the back burner. Prioritizing human connection is paramount to a full mind body connection. We are animals designed to connect. Make physical and emotional intimacy a priority by scheduling moments for closeness, initiate conversations about your desires, and stay tuned in to your partner's needs. Intimacy is a crucial aspect of thriving relationships. Social interactions are also essential. Make time for friends, participate in a hobby, attend sporting events or concerts. These connections provide support and moments of relaxation in the mid of life's demands.

And back to the whole point of this book….don't forget to carve out time for yourself. You time is vital for self-care and rejuvenation. A lot of people will look at self-care as selfish but it couldn't be any further from the truth. It is a necessary component of maintaining balance and as you continue on your meditation through movement journey, these moments of you time will be everything.

To truly balance various aspects of life requires a realistic understanding of your own limitations and a commitment to consistency. That's it. Set realistic expectations, understand that cannot be perfect in every role you play. Perfectionism can lead to burnout and dissatisfaction. Accept that there will always be ups and downs, and not only is it normal, but our lifelong pursuit is to better navigate those ups and downs, not eliminate them. Life is about dealing with what comes at us in the most effective way possible, not being perfect and comfortable all the time. Stay focused on progress and effort rather than unattainable perfection. Consistency is key to maintaining balance. Create routines and stick to them as closely as possible. Consistency provides stability and predictability, reducing stress and chaos in your daily life. Regular routines can also help you allocate time more effectively. Meditation is all about consistency and not only does it get easier over time, it also becomes more effective. While consistency is important, it's equally crucial to remain flexible. Life is unpredictable and at some point unexpected events will disrupt your plans. Embrace flexibility and adapt to these changes without feeling overwhelmed. This adaptability will make the juggling act more manageable.

In the forever quest for balance, it's vital to remember that you can only do what you can. There are limits to your time, energy, and resources. Accepting these limitations with grace is an essential part of maintaining balance. Prioritize your responsibilities based on their urgency and importance. Some tasks may require your immediate attention, while others can wait. By focusing on what matters most at any given moment, you can make the best use of your time. You also don't have to do everything alone. Seek support from family, friends, or professional resources when needed. What's the point of having family and friends if we never lean on them? Just as much as we're bettering ourselves to be there for others, there is people in your life ready and willing to be there for you. Don't be afraid to lean on the people in your life when you're needing some extra support. Be kind to yourself. Understand that it's normal to have moments of imbalance. Forgive yourself when you fall short, and avoid self-criticism. Self-compassion is a powerful tool for maintaining mental and emotional well-being and essential to further your meditation journey.

Finding balance in the juggle of life is an ongoing process that requires intention and effort. By setting boundaries, defining priorities, maintaining realistic expectations, and understanding your limits, you can navigate the complexities of work, family, relationships, and personal well-being. Remember that it's not about achieving a perfect balance but rather about continuously striving for progress in the ever-evolving dance of life.

5

You Are Strong

When you think of strength, what does that mean to you? Is it a certain weight goal? Is it a specific activity? Is it endurance? No, seriously, what does that mean to you? I want you to think about it and answer it out loud. Hear yourself say it. Is it reasonable? Is it something that you can actually work towards and achieve? Similar to meditation, strength can mean whatever we want it to. We're often bombarded by media images of the "ideal body" when the reality is the people we're seeing are professionals. They get paid to adhere to strict diets and exercise regimens. Having a six pack or running a marathon is not the only definition of strength. Redefine what strength is for you and make that a regular visualization on your journey. For me, strength is the ability to do whatever I want to do without feeling inadequate. Sometimes that means going on a multi-day hike or trying to push my endurance limits with a long run. But more often than not, it means being able to enjoy a day swimming with my wife and dogs or enjoying a 30 minute yoga session. This is a concept known as functional strength. As we age, endurance and the ability to do for ourselves is everything. When we align our minds with our movements we start to listen when our bodies speak to us. Our bodies tell us when they feel tension, when they feel stagnant, when they feel relaxed. Developing an awareness to that connection builds confidence in our abilities and stamina.

You are strong. You've already accomplished so many things in life that just a brief time ago you thought were impossible. Recognize and remind yourself of those accomplishments. Big and small, every single one matters and got you where you are today. Strength comes in many forms; emotional, physical, spiritual; recognize the strength you already have and building on it won't seem quite as scary. You are strong. You are resilient. When you take the time to listen to your body, you are meditating through movement. Those repetitive actions, performed with awareness, is exactly what this is all about. Pay attention. Be aware. Make adjustments.

The majority of strength comes from the mind. Have you ever heard a story about seemingly impossible strength? When our bodies perform at a high capacity, it's because the mind is allowing it to. Our minds control every single action we take and a strong mind will trickle down to all the things you experience in life. It requires a strong mind to build physical strength yet it doesn't require physical strength to build a strong mind. That gives me insight to the importance of a strong mind. I mentioned before that meditation acts as an exercise for the mind. Small, consistent, repetitive actions over time build strength. Getting lost in movement of any kind is meditative practice in one of its best forms. Exercise your mind. Exercise your body. You are Strong. Mental strength equals physical strength and you cannot have one without the other.

One of our primary goals of meditative practice is finding that connection between body and mind. How you feel matters and I promise you that when you feel strong, things around you seem easy. When you're mentally strong anxiety and stress feel less evident and full of doom. We feel confident that we have the strength to tackle whatever is thrown in our path. Mental strength is one of the most valuable tools in our survival arsenal. There will be extremely challenging moments in all of our lives and 9 times out of 10, those moments won't require physical strength. However, feeling physical strong is also a guaranteed mental and confidence booster. Exercising our minds and our bodies set the stage for all other activities and responsibilities in life. It makes us better partners, parents, colleagues, and ultimately better individuals. You are strong.

6

Exploring Various Meditative Movements

So what type of movements are the best meditative practices? Well ultimately that's for you to decide and as you further yourself down a path of personal connection and self awareness, questions like these will become easier and easier to answer. But for our purposes, I figured I'd share a few of my favorites.

Around my mid twenties, when I was starting to pull myself out of my funk, an older friend and mentor was actively attending yoga. He's probably 25 years older than me and after years of back issues was suddenly feeling better than I'd seen him in years. He invited me to a yoga class and it was basically love at first sight. Throughout my twenties I truly found a love of yoga. It is maybe the ultimate expression of meditative movement. There is breath work, visualization, mantras, body scanning, and of course strength building. So many of those concepts could be a singular meditative focus in itself but with yoga, you're forced to combine multiple disciplines at once with complete awareness.

I still continue to include yoga as a regular part of my life. I find it particularly useful when I feel stagnant in multiple areas. When I feel unmotivated to workout or focus, yoga gives me a moment to recenter almost without thinking about it. I fully identify as a person with an over active mind and quieting that noise has been one of my biggest personal challenges in my meditative journey. Because yoga is so demanding of multiple disciplines, when I really focus at the task at hand of aligning breath with movement, all of a sudden I notice my mind is clear.

Now, like I've said in several other ways, yoga is what you want it to be. A lot of us have an idealized image or association with yoga of being for attractive young hippies with perfect bodies and unrealistic flexibility. Don't forget what we learned in Chapter 3! Set realistic expectations and be consistent. The beauty of yoga is that every single move or position can be modified to your comfort, strength, and flexibility. I'm always so inspired when I see someone in their twilight years still working on their strength and flexibility, engaging their minds and muscles. Yoga can be suitable for any age, body type, or background and especially now more than ever. Thanks to YouTube, there are countless yoga videos and instructors and I feel confident you can find something that suits your needs. Start small, be realistic, be consistent and you will see improvement in yourself in a variety of ways. Yoga is one of the easiest ways to become more aware and in tune with your body and inner self.

My first introduction to meditation, before I even knew the word meditation, was martial arts. Growing up a massive fan of Ninja Turtles and watching old black and white reruns of martial arts movies it was a no brainer for my parents to sign me up for classes. What I had no idea is that I's be learning to move my body with intention and extreme focus. Martial arts is completely about the power of the mind. It's about the small guy being able to defend himself against the big guy with focus and mental strength. It's about knowing yourself and having the confidence to walk away from a fight not walk towards it. And I'm not just talking about a physical fight. We fight mental battles every single day and martial arts is a practice that forces us to quiet the mind, breath, and focus. It is one of the oldest and most practiced traditions in the world. There's a reason that there's entire convents of monks living and training together. They aren't training for battle, they're training for spirituality.

There are all kinds of disciplines that fall under martial arts. The ones I have the most experience with are Tae Kwon Do, Karate, and Kung Fu. All three are very prevalent in this country and have a strict focus on the connection of body and mind. If you've ever heard of the concept of Chi, it's essentially the alignment of the physical and metaphysical, or mind, body and spirit. Martial arts is a focus on the power of Chi, how to manifest it, how to be one with it. A consistent practice will open you to a whole world of meditative movement.

The form of meditative movement that is closest to my heart and ultimately defines who I am is dance. Specifically dance as expression. I haven't mentioned this yet but in my daily life, I'm a professional musician. A drummer to be precise. The natural rhythm of the world has fascinated me since before I could walk. I can hear, see, and recognize patterns in the most unassuming of scenarios. With that comes a love of dance. And I don't mean two stepping. Dance as expression is what ever you want it to be. It's likely what you do when no-one is watching you. Releasing ourselves to rhythm and music can boost our mood and alleviate stress and anxiety. So many of us turn towards music when we're feeling sad or down. It has the power to lift us up and make us whole again. Losing yourself in dance is an amazing way to regenerate your spirit while actively moving your body. Being aware of rhythm and getting lost in it is one of my great joys in life.

In some of my worst times, I'd spend hours a day playing the drums. Maybe even the same simple rhythm over and over and over again. It would allow a brief moment of respite from the anxiety and depression I was feeling at the time. Those moments I had sticks in my hands, everything else disappeared. It's a fully immersive meditative state with a singular focus. In recent years, several organizations have started using drum therapy for everything from addiction and trauma to autism (4,5). There has proven to be a direct correlation with drumming and positive effects on brain function and behavior in young people with autism (5).

Of course not everyone can drum or has access to drums, but everyone and anyone can dance and the feeling of getting lost in movement with rhythm can have a similar uplifting effect on your body and mind. Turn on your favorite groovy track and move your body. Get lost in it. Put it on repeat and keep dancing. Flail your arms. Shake your hair. Get weird with it and move your body!

The one movement that everyone talks about wanting to do but equally hates is running. It can be hard on the joints and truly feels like a task. At risk of sounding like a broken record, start small and be consistent. Running doesn't have to be about speed or distance but just getting out there and doing it. If you've ever heard of a "runner's high", that's the moment when all of a sudden your breath, your pulse, and your body relax. The moment before you were likely hating life and your choices and all of a sudden you feel powerful. The same things can be achieved from consistent walking. Taking repetitive steps with breath alignment is one of the best things we can do for functional strength. Seniors who walk daily are shown to have better overall health and general satisfaction with their lives. When we ad breath to that movement, we hone our focus and it becomes meditation.

When I'm traveling around the country on tour with my band, I'm always searching for a nice place to go on a run, walk, or hike. Getting outside and spending 30 minutes to an hour with myself feels like a full body regeneration. When I'm feeling homesick or lonely, spending time appreciating my surroundings and my body and where I'm at physically and emotionally, is a reminder that I'm where I'm supposed to be. Force yourself to go outside and walk or run, take in your surroundings and eventually you may realize that while your body is moving, your mind becomes still. Moving in stillness is a true harmony of meditative movement. Our bodies are being physical and taking on the load while our minds are still and calm. As always, start small and be consistent. Progress is always a product of repetition and discipline.

Be curious, explore, try new things and don't be afraid to

fail. Half the battle is getting out there and making the effort. Eventually find the type of movement that brings you the most peace and make it a part of who you are. Movement isn't a task but a reward. A reward for all the handwork we put in and all the responsibilities we juggle. Taking time for yourself to move and realign within, is one of the best gifts you can give yourself. And don't forget, you are strong!

7

Mindful Meditative Techniques

I've mentioned various ways we can get closer to mindful movement across several chapters but here we'll discuss some specific types of meditative practices you can do to start your journey.

The first and most important is breath awareness. I've touched on it across several chapters but I really can't stress the importance enough. It's one of the few things we do 24/7 and so many of us are completely unaware of the activity and feeling. There are several ways to bring breath awareness into your life from relaxing to wildly intense. I'm just going to touch on a few of the more calming techniques here but if you start to really enjoy breath work, I encourage you to do more research on your own and find a technique that fits your needs and goals.

A very simple and always accessible technique is **pursed lip breathing**. You can do this several times a day and in just a few minutes you can reset your mind and feel relief from the load you're carrying. To do it:

1. Sit in a relaxed position
2. With your lips closed, inhale through your nose for 2 seconds
3. Keeping your lips together exhale slowly exhale for 4 seconds and repeat

That's it! Simple enough, right? Congratulations, you just became more breath aware! This practice can be done quickly in just a few minutes or you can sit with it for 30 minutes or longer. It's a very accessible and effective entry into breath work and breath awareness.

Another technique I really enjoy is **alternate nostril breathing**. This type of breath has been shown to improve cardiovascular function and lower your heart rate. If your feeling stuffy or congested it's provably not the best time to try this one as it's easiest performed when your not fighting anything coming out.

1. Sit in a comfortable position
2. Raise your hand toward your nose and use your right thumb to close your right nostril
3. Inhale through your left nostril, then press it closed with your index finger
4. Remove your thumb and exhale out through your right nostril
5. Inhale through your right nostril and press it closed with your thumb
6. Remove your index finger to open your left nostril and exhale
7. That is one complete cycle
8. Repeat this pattern for up to 5 minutes

9. End your breath work with an exhale on the left side

Concentrate on keeping your breath even and steady with a similar amount of time focused on each inhale and exhale.

One of my favorites and maybe one of the most popular breathing exercises is **deep breathing**. A lot of us have already practiced some version of this in our lives. Even if your closest memory is a parent telling you, "pause and take a deep breath," when you were just a kid letting your emotions get the best of you. Deep breathing is a very grounding and centering practice that I try to make a daily part of my life. To effectively focus on deep breath:

1. Find that comfortable position whether seated or standing with a nice upright posture
2. Inhale as deep as you can through your nose
3. Hold your breath for 5 seconds
4. Slowly exhale through your nose

These are just a few of my favorites and some of the easiest for beginners, but again, feel free to explore other techniques on your own. Schedule some amount of time a few days a week to sit and perform a brief breath exercise. Of course always consult with your doctor if you have any personal issues or concerns but in general these exercises are noninvasive and extremely low risk. Regular breath work is a great gateway into the world of meditative movement. (5)

One of the reasons I enjoy yoga so much is it forces me to actively work on body scanning. **Body scanning** is the process of bringing awareness to every part of your body in a gradually ascending manner. Starting with your toes and working all the way up to your head, the idea is to give a moment of complete focus, awareness, and intention to each part of your body before moving on to the next. By focusing on that connection, you become aware of all the tense and achy muscles, inflamed or painful joints, and any other discomfort you may be feeling. This exercise is entirely about awareness and not relief or pain management.

So how do we effectively perform a body scan? Like all the types of meditation we've been discussing, a body scan is intended to be accessible and easy for all persons.

1. Always start all meditation by making yourself comfortable. Body Scans are best performed lying down so roll out a yoga mat or some sort of cushion and get comfy. I recommend avoiding your bed and finding a balance between firm and soft to make sure your spine keeps alignment.

2. Begin by doing a breath deep breathing exercise, really focusing on your diaphragm and deep belly breaths. Try to avoid using your chest and shoulders and really breath into your belly, filling it with as much air as you can. After a few deep breaths, slow it down and fall into a natural mindful breath pattern.

3. First notice your feet. Feel each one of your toes, the arches, your heels and ankles. What sensations do you feel? Recognize any tension and visualize sending your breath to that area of your body. After a few breaths keep working up through your calves, knees, thighs, and so on.

Taking each moment to think about that specific body part and only that body part. Notice how it feels and recognize what it needs. If anything feels uncomfortable, pause and breath into it before moving on. Imagine the tension dissipating from your body and returning to a completely relaxed state.

4. Move up your entire body all the way to your head. Take a moment to reevaluate everything you just felt and experienced. Hone in on the awareness you just created and store it in your memory for easier accessibility in the future. As we work on this practice, we awaken to body awareness in our everyday lives. When you start to realize why it is the way you feel, you can start to work on correcting it and being your most capable self. (6)

Body scanning, when properly executed, should leave you feeling very relaxed and rejuvenated. It can alleviate mental stress and almost feel like you just woke up from the perfectly restorative nap. Make sure to modify to your needs, whether it be body position or limited time, even a brief scan can further you on your journey.

Visualization is a powerful method employed by people from all walks of life to calm the mind, inject positivity into our lives, and work towards our goals and desires. Adults notoriously struggle with an active imagination and visualization can help expand that part of your mind. Think of a child blissfully playing with an imaginary friend or with imaginary objects. They're so happy and in the moment that whatever it is they're doing feels completely real and tangible. Tapping into that can bring us all kinds of different fulfillment from physical manifestations to pulling ourselves out of crushing anxiety before it takes over. Visualization can train our subconscious to work towards our goals even when we might not be readily thinking about it.

There's two main types of visualization. Outcome visualization is imagining a specific goal or finish line. For example, seeing yourself cross the finish line of a marathon or getting big job promotion. You're focusing on designing a specific moment or achievement. The other is process visualization. If your outcome is finishing that 26.2 miles, how are you going to get there? You can't just see end and instantly teleport yourself to that point in time. You still have to live through every second, minute, and hour it takes to get there. Process visualization is seeing all the steps you'll need to take to get there. When combining both outcome and process we start developing a clear vision and path to get to where we want in life.

Visualization is about creating the environment you want to exist in. In life we get to choose to respond to the world around us, or engage with it and mold it to what we want. Something I've said for a long time is life is a game and we're playing whether we choose to or not. You either learn the rules and compete or you get played and are just a pawn in someone else's story. Visualization techniques not only help us learn the rules but write them as well. We get to build the foundations of our true desires and goals and exist within that parameter. Much of life is based on our perception. As you work on visualizing the world you want all of a sudden you'll realize you're already living in it.

As a performer on stage in front of thousands of people, I spent years seeing myself in that position before I ever even knew it was possible. From a young age I'd spent time seeing myself as a professional musician and drummer that I couldn't possibly imagine anything else. Even when I was living other lives and pursuing other endeavors, it was still there. It wasn't until I was 30 years old that I fully leaned towards a life of music, touring the country and playing to countless fans. Before music, I worked hanging window coverings, spraying insulation in attics and crawlspaces, delivering cupcakes, landscaping in the Texas summers and through all of it I identified as a drummer and musician first. I played every day, performed when I could, and inserted myself in the Austin, TX music scene. I wasn't fully aware at the time but I was actively living in process visualization while obsessing over outcome visualization. Knowing what you want and how to get there is paramount to being in tune with our minds, bodies, and spirits.

Like with all these techniques, follow a simple process and expand on it as you continue to practice.

1. Can you guess yet? Get comfortable! Sit, lay down, recline, whatever feels right in the moment.
2. Close your eyes and start with a few deep breaths, pausing at the top of the inhale with a long slow release.
3. Begin to imagine the environment you want to exist in. Be specific. What does it sound like? What does it look like? How does it smell and taste? Engage your senses and really try to feel them. Add as much detail to the environment around you as possible.
4. Focus on the emotion this space creates. How does it make

you feel? The more you can feel what that space is like, the closer you get to it becoming a reality. Place yourself there so vividly that when it happens it's already a familiar feeling.

5. Stay there for as long as you'd like. When it's time to return, slowly reengage focus on your breath and use it as a bridge back into the real world. Batting your eyes open and processing everything you just felt.

Make time for this process a few times a week. And remember that it doesn't have to be performed completely on it's own. A lot of these methods can be combined and engaged in at the same time. You can be breathing mindfully while actively a body scanning and visualizing your goals. The more harmony we find in the process the more it becomes an intuitive second nature. (7)

8

Meditative Movement in Daily Life

One of the most life changing experiences for me is working meditative movement into my daily activities and routines. There's several moments throughout our day that we can pause and incorporate awareness into our responsibilities and rituals. You can think about your breath when you're brushing your teeth. You can visualize and body scan while you're prepping dinner and cutting vegetables. Find moments in your day that can be more than just the activity at hand. Managing our daily load and taking control of it will alleviate stress and anxiety, making us feel less like a pawn and more actively engaged in our outcomes.

Morning rituals are one of the easiest ways to build consistency into your routine. You could start a body scan as soon as you wake up. Or take the dogs on a walk before breakfast and practice your breath and steady pacing. It doesn't have to be a big to do and it doesn't have to take a lot of time. Even 5 minutes of dedication when you start your day will help boost your mood and prep you for the daily load ahead of you. Being consistent and refusing to let the anxiety and stress control us first thing in the morning will help ease a bit of the pressure you feel throughout your day. A morning meditation can be just as important for your body as breakfast. Think of it as breakfast for your mind. Give it a little nourishment and you're likely to have more energy and positivity for the rest of your day.

If getting out of bed isn't the hardest part of the day, going back to work after lunch is a strong contender. The mid day crash affects almost all of us and rarely do we have time for a little siesta pick me up. Instead of heading back to the coffee station or chugging a red bull, you can achieve some midday revitalization with a quick meditation. Work an extra five minutes into your schedule where you can sit in your car or close your office door and check in with yourself. Close your eyes and set a timer, just in case that siesta does come for you. Align your breath, do a body scan, visualize your goals. A brief check in will re-energize and help get you through the final hump of the day.

Probably the most important time of the day for some sort of meditation and movement is in the evening. If you work in an office, you've been sitting and staring at a computer all day and your body is likely feeling achy and stagnant. Maybe you work a labor job and your muscles and joints are feeling worn out. At the end of the day we're carrying all the stress and tension we've built up throughout the day and shedding it before sleep is crucial to a full nights rest. When you get home from work, it's a perfect time for some mindful movement. Do a quick yoga video, stretch, go on a walk, maybe go to the gym for a more intense workout. Do what your body wants and needs and if you've been consistent in your practice, you'll know exactly what that is. When we feel over worked, light movement or stretching and breath work will calm your aches and pains and quiet the chatter in your head. And when we're feeling stagnant, movement will wake up your muscles and get blood flowing to all your vital organs including your brain, stimulating your mind and imagination. Turning off and detaching from the work and responsibilities and looking forward to tomorrow will make you feel more well rounded and fulfilled, forcing you to remember that there is life outside of work and responsibility. Spend time with your family, cook dinner, be actively present with yourself and your people. Move your body and be mindful.

Every day we're confronted with a new set of challenges and stresses. Sometimes we can expect and anticipate them and sometimes they're from the complete unknown. Managing stress is a constant pursuit. I know I sound like a broken record but your journey should too. By that I mean repeat the process and be consistent. The more we lean into these different methods, the easier it is for stress to melt away and not be in control. A healthy mind and healthy body are the best tools in our arsenal for the daily battle of life. As personal challenges arise the best thing you can do is pause and breath. Clear minds lead to better decisions and better decisions lead to better potential outcomes. The whole point is setting ourselves up for the best possible chance at success. We deal with so many factors that are completely out of our control and by focusing on the things we can control, we build the confidence we need to handle the uncontrollable.

When I lost my father I truly felt like I'd lost my own life as well. And I wasn't entirely wrong I just didn't have to right perspective. I lost the life I'd known but I was also opened to a new life that I didn't quite yet understand. Trauma and tragedy is as guaranteed as rain. It's not going to happen everyday, and sometimes there's a long drought, but every once in a while you deal with a complete downpour and flood. Daily meditation and movement is training for these moments even when we don't know it. The stronger our minds and bodies, the better we handle our weakest most challenging moments. Exercise, practice, and consistency are the best habits we can build and the more we build them the better we manage stress and anxiety.

These practices can also relieve a creatively stagnant mind. As a creative it's sometimes crushing to know what to do next or where to go. There's no boss setting goals, deadlines, and expectations for you. There's no process to follow or software to do the work for you. Creatives have to be masters of visualization. The whole process starts with seeing a finish line that doesn't even exist and the the process of who to get there. I don't know a single creative that isn't directly benefited from meditation and mindful movement practices. Strengthening imagination and connecting with ourselves aid in expression and production. Not only will it unlock ideas and possibilities but you'll also increase your ability to give your full attention and focus to the task at hand. Creatives should constantly work on becoming masters of the mind to unlock their full potential.

Society tends to hold an idealized version of the tortured genius creative on a pedestal but personally I don't find that mentality to be a healthy and sustainable approach. A lot of the people we associate those qualities with tend to burn bright and quick and struggle with their place in society and within themselves. That's one of the reasons we lose a lot of them so young. I believe that being a creative can be a sustainable life long practice without sacrificing authenticity. There is nothing inauthentic about focusing within and aligning mind, body, and spirit. If you are consistent in your practice and journey, you will unlock creative potential with an ease that you didn't know was possible. You will also be more productive with your time and the effort it takes to achieve your goals. Be consistent. Be patient. Be realistic. You are strong.

9

Finding Consistency

I've said the word 'consistent' countless times in previous chapters and guess what? For the sake of being consistent, we're still talking about it. Consistency is something we struggle with in a large variety of ways. Yo-yo dieting, fad exercise routines, starting and quitting hobbies, never learning another language, whatever it is we've all started down a path and at some point quit. What made you stop? Did you feel inadequate or incapable? Did the rewards start to not seem worth it? Were our expectations unrealistic? Did your goals change halfway through? The main reason we don't achieve our goals and attain the things we want is because we stop trying. To me success is the refusal to quit. I genuinely believe that. Of course there's always exceptions to the rule and some things are worth quitting. You don't want to keep your self in a bad or potentially detrimental position just because. But when we really want something all you have to do is keep trying. That persistence and consistency has given you everything you have. From learning how to read to driving a car, buying a house or landing a new gig. At some point you've completed a million small tasks and actions to achieve one specific goal. Apply that same logic to meditation and movement and you'll be on your way to a better more aligned you.

Realistic goals are the most important part. Write down your goals. Let yourself look at it and analyze if it's real or not. Winning the lottery is not a goal, but financial literacy is. You don't plan for retirement by working on one huge payday at some random point in time. You're store a way a few dollars here and there for years and decades, slowly making progress toward your goal. Everything we want in life is achieved that exact same way. When you write down your goals think about the small things you can do to get there and then write those down as well. Those small actions are the real goals. Getting out of bed the next day and doing something that gets you further down that path. The real goal is in the process not the end game. Become addicted to the process. Get obsessed with the process. Find the smallest thing you can define and do that. The best part about focusing on the process, or as I like to call them 'mini-goals', is you're constantly achieving. You get to complete tasks and feel pride in yourself. When we feel proud of ourselves, it's so much easier to keep pushing forward with our actions. Focus on the process and set mini-goals and the larger goals will be right in front of you.

Don't forget to track your progress. Goals and process don't mean much if you aren't aware of the fact that you're getting there. Find a system that works for you and stick with it. You can make some sort of spreadsheet with specific times and actions or it can be more free form like a daily journal. Just something that allows you to check in with yourself and not rely on memory for everything you've done. As time goes by it will also act as a confidence booster. You'll be able to go back, see where you started, and recognize how far you've come. Tracking your progress not only creates accountability but also increases morale. Enable yourself to plainly see the improvement you're achieving.

As important as it is to hold ourselves accountable, it's equally important to build a support system with your friends, family and mentors. Talk to them about your journey, your goals, and your process. Check in with them every once in a while to let them know how you're doing. Lean on people when you need support and ask for encouragement when you feel unmotivated. Don't be afraid to ask for help from the people around you. Most of the time our closest circle is eager and willing to give us the support we need if they just knew we needed it. It's also important to surround ourselves with people we look up to. People that may have more experience or wisdom and understand where we are and where we're coming from are crucial to helping us on our journey. Mentors are great for inspiring us to keep moving forward and showing us what we could become. Surround yourself with inspiration and motivation. Seeing that it's possible for other people will make you believe that it's possible for you too. All good things are achieved with time, focus and consistency. Be realistic and stick with it. You are strong!

10

Transforming Your Life Through Meditative Movement

Meditative movement, performed with consistency and intention, can transform your life in so many different areas you'll forget what it was like before you started. Cultivate a deeper connection to yourself and learn what you need. Flip your thinking and take control of your goals and desires instead of leaving it up to chance. Find the movement or variety of movements that work for you and make it a habitual part of your every day life. Check in with yourself, mind and body, daily and be honest about what you feel. Remember, this is about creating a process and a lifelong pursuit. There is no such thing as perfection and I promise you, you'll be far from it. What you can be is a little better today than you were yesterday and a little more focused, confident, and stronger tomorrow than you are today.

Get out there and try. As they say, variety is the spice of life. Mix up the types of movement you do and meditation you practice. Dabble in the experiences of life and peace and happiness will be somewhere in the mix. The importance of nurturing personal growth can't be stated strongly enough. Actively trying to better ourselves mentally and physically will make you a better you for yourself and your loved ones. So many opportunities and experiences will open themselves up to you that you may not have been fit enough or in the right mindset to recognize previously. There's always opportunity swirling around us and we just have to be confident enough in ourselves to seize the moment. Move your body and be aware of your breath. Feel your muscles and feel your emotions. The benefits of one will benefit the other.

Be proud of yourself and be kind to yourself. You are strong and capable. You are intelligent and confident. You are not perfect and you are not superhuman. We expect the world from ourselves and the world expects even more of us. At the end of the day all we can do is what we can. Be honest about your limitations and don't beat yourself up about them. Know yourself, know your limits, and push yourself with kindness and empathy for your own needs. Recognize the milestones and accomplishments you achieve and feel proud. Find ways to reward yourself. It doesn't have to be crazy or expensive. A bubble bath, an ice cream cone on a Tuesday, a walk when autumn finally hits, rewards can come in all shapes and sizes. It doesn't matter what you choose but the act of self reward is just another thing that continues to build that foundation of confidence and self connection.

If not a physical reward, just take some time to celebrate your journey. Look back on your tracking and see how far you've come. Recognize where you are and how good it feels. If we don't take a moment to pause and reward ourselves, we can get lost in the reason we're doing what we're doing in the first place. At the end of the day it's all about improving how we feel by activating our mind and body. Little moments of reward will keep you excited about the journey and help maintain that consistency. Be confident in your achievements and congratulate yourself. You are strong and you deserve it.

Finally, share your experience with others. For most of us, it's very hard to talk about ourselves without feeling like we're bragging or being self centered. But when we share our struggles and our successes, other people may be inspired to start the journey themselves. We're all here for the first time doing the best we can and so many things seem impossible at first until we see someone else experiencing and overcoming similar challenges. Your accomplishments might encourage someone else to continue their journey or maybe you even become a mentor to someone just starting. Share the hard challenging times and share the success and achievements. All you are is an imperfect human and all you can do is try to be a little better everyday.

Now get out there, move your body and activate your mind! Your life is your experience and yours alone. It's up to you how you want to exist and participate in that experience. Meditation in movement is an amazing tool to better know yourself and your body. Exercise your mind with your body for true functional strength and everything from stress and anxiety to joint pain and depression will start to become more manageable. Giving ourselves attention and dedication is so important to a well rounded and wholesome lifestyle. I hope you feel inspired to continue your meditative movement journey and unlock your best inner self, reduce stress, improve confidence and well-being, and transform your life for the better. Onward!

11

Resources

1. Mindfulness meditation: A research-proven way to reduce stress. Published October 30, 2019. Accessed October 12, 2023. *https://www.apa.org*. https://www.apa.org/topics/mindfulness/meditation#:~:text=Researchers%20reviewed%20more%20than%20200,%2C%20pain%2C%20smoking%20and%20addiction.

2. Harvard Health. Meditation and a relaxation technique to lower blood pressure. Harvard Health. Published July 18, 2023. Accessed October 12, 2023. https://www.health.harvard.edu/heart-health/meditation-and-a-relaxation-technique-to-lower-blood-pressure#:~:text=A%20number%20of%20well%2Ddesigned,published%20in%20the%20journal%20Hypertension

3. Rea S. Neurobiological changes explain how mindfulness meditation improves health - News - Carnegie Mellon University. Carnegie Mellon University. Published February 4, 2016. Accessed October 12, 2023. https://www.cm

u.edu/news/stories/archives/2016/february/meditation-changes-brain.html#:~:text=The%20biological%20health%2Drelated%20benefits,explain%20the%20improvements%20in%20inflammation

4. Treatment AA. Learn how drum therapy helps relieve stress and anxiety in treatment. *Ashley Addiction Treatment.* Published online February 21, 2020. Accessed October 12, 2023. https://www.ashleytreatment.org/rehab-blog/how-drum-therapy-can-benefit-recovery/#:~:text=Drum%20therapy%20encourages%20people%20to,on%20an%20even%20playing%20field

5. Cronkleton E. 10 breathing techniques for stress relief and more. Healthline. Published March 24, 2023. Accessed October 13, 2023. https://www.healthline.com/health/breathing-exercise#alternate-nostril-breathing

6. Scott E PhD. Body Scan meditation. Verywell Mind. Published online September 13, 2021. Accessed October 13, 2023. https://www.verywellmind.com/body-scan-meditation-why-and-how-3144782#:~:text=Body%20scanning%20involves%20paying%20attention,%2C%20tension%2C%20or%20general%20discomfort

7. Moe K. 5 visualization techniques to help you reach your goals. BetterUp. Published June 4, 2021. Accessed October 13, 2023. https://www.betterup.com/blog/visualization